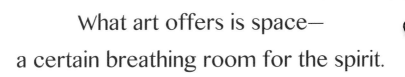

What art offers is space—
a certain breathing room for the spirit.

—John Updike

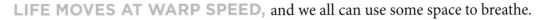

LIFE MOVES AT WARP SPEED, and we all can use some space to breathe.

Many of us are masters of multitasking—masters of doing—so it's difficult to slow down and just *be*. And we're constantly immersed in technology and dinging digital devices demanding our attention, making it difficult to unplug.

Coloring offers an enjoyable way to slow down and reconnect with your creative, playful side. Remember as a kid spending hours coloring with a big box of crayons? In that same way, many adults are losing themselves in coloring because it's restorative to their spirits.

Coloring instills a sense of peace. It allows you to free your mind of worries and focus your attention on the present moment, which leads to a state of mindfulness. And—it turns out—coloring is good for your mind, your body, and your soul.

Mindfulness is about being fully awake in our lives.
It is about perceiving the exquisite
vividness of each moment.

—Jon Kabat-Zinn

While it can take years to fully master mindfulness, it begins with intention. Being more mindful means acting with more kindness and compassion (even toward ourselves), slowing down to enjoy the simple moments, accepting the moment as it is, and seeing the beauty in the ordinary.

Mindfulness is the aware, balanced acceptance of the present experience. It is opening to or receiving the present moment, pleasant or unpleasant, just as it is, without either clinging to it or rejecting it.

—Sylvia Boorstein

Coloring is a perfect exercise in mindfulness. It's not about producing a perfect page; it's about slowing down, connecting to the moment, and taking time to let go and create without being attached to the outcome.

Illustrator Judy Clement Wall designed each page in this book to instill a sense of relaxation. You'll find several mandalas, which have been used in many cultures and therapeutic settings to help quiet the mind. You'll also find a range of designs, from simpler ones that can be colored in less time to more intricate patterned pages. Each image is paired with a quote that conveys a key principle of living mindfully, from acceptance to awareness, from compassion to letting go, from quieting the mind to being open to new possibilities.

Almost everything will work again if you unplug it for a few minutes . . . including you.

—Anne Lamott

May the quotes and images inspire you to savor each moment and find a restorative way to recharge so you can make each day a masterpiece.

Unplug, unwind, and let your artistry bloom.

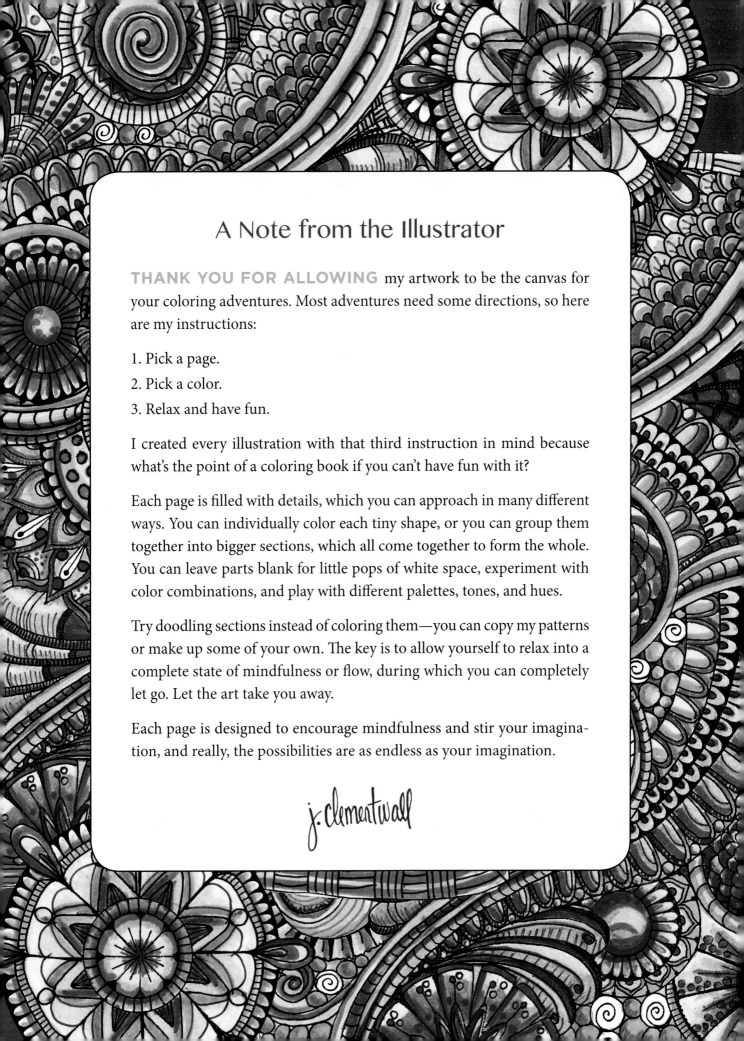

A Note from the Illustrator

THANK YOU FOR ALLOWING my artwork to be the canvas for your coloring adventures. Most adventures need some directions, so here are my instructions:

1. Pick a page.
2. Pick a color.
3. Relax and have fun.

I created every illustration with that third instruction in mind because what's the point of a coloring book if you can't have fun with it?

Each page is filled with details, which you can approach in many different ways. You can individually color each tiny shape, or you can group them together into bigger sections, which all come together to form the whole. You can leave parts blank for little pops of white space, experiment with color combinations, and play with different palettes, tones, and hues.

Try doodling sections instead of coloring them—you can copy my patterns or make up some of your own. The key is to allow yourself to relax into a complete state of mindfulness or flow, during which you can completely let go. Let the art take you away.

Each page is designed to encourage mindfulness and stir your imagination, and really, the possibilities are as endless as your imagination.

j. clementwall

Coloring Tools and Tips

COLORED PENCILS: With a variety of shapes and sizes, colored pencils are great for shading or blending colors together, both of which add interest and depth to any design.

GEL PENS AND MARKERS: Magic markers and gel pens are good for adding bold, defined bursts of color.

CRAYONS: A staple of any household with kids, crayons are surprisingly versatile when filling in large spaces.

TIP: Add a piece of scrap paper under each page you're working on to make sure that the color doesn't bleed through the page.

Choose Your Colors

You can use both complementary and analogous colors to make a gorgeous piece of art—the possibilities are as endless as your imagination.

PRIMARY COLORS

The primary colors—red, yellow, and blue—are denoted by a "P" on the outside of the color wheel. Primary colors cannot be created by mixing any other colors.

SECONDARY COLORS

The secondary colors—green, orange, and purple—are shown by an "S" on the color wheel. These are formed by mixing the primary colors.

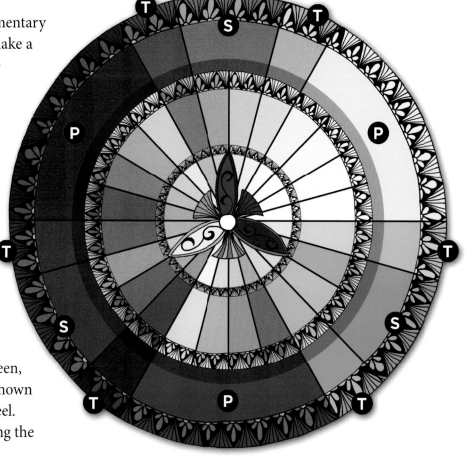

TERTIARY COLORS

Yellow-orange, red-orange, red-purple, blue-purple, blue-green, and yellow-green make up the tertiary colors, which are noted with a "T" on the outside of the wheel. These colors are formed by mixing a primary color with a secondary color.

Inspiration Is All Around You

Not sure what colors to use? You can find a rainbow of inspiration all around you in your daily life. Take a few minutes each day to look and to really notice the patterns of different plants and animals, the colors of the flowers that dot your street, and the radiant hues of the sunset or the morning sky. By being more mindful of the colors that make up your day, you can make them come alive in your own creations. Get inspired by the designs on the following page, too. As you can see, each artist lends his or her own style and personality to the artwork. One person may choose sunny yellows, another may pick soft teals, and another will add background doodles. There is no right way or wrong way to approach any page—the key is to enjoy the moment and your unique creations that result!

1 PIECE OF ART, 3 DIFFERENT INTERPRETATIONS

warm sunny colors

Marker art by Christine Belleris

subtle shading

Colored pencil art by Kevin Stawieray

cool colors

Crayon art by Lori Golden

Marker art by Robyn Henoch

Crayon art by Dawn Grove

Gel pen art by Kim Weiss

Marker and colored pencil art by Robyn Henoch

Marker and colored pencil art by Robyn Henoch

Marker and colored pencil art by Robyn Henoch

Marker art by Kevin Stawieray

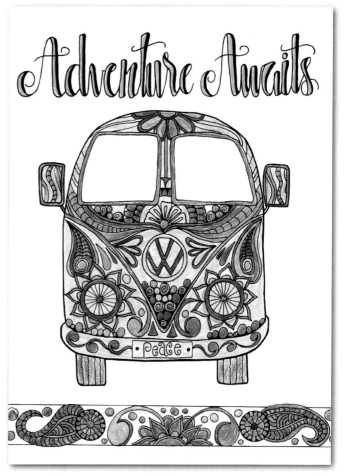

Crayon art by Dawn Grove

Colored pencil art by Linda Schneider, winner of the Mindful Living Adult Coloring Contest
sponsored by HCI, AARP, and the City of Boynton Beach Art in Public Places program

Write it on your heart that every day

is the best day in the year.

—Ralph Waldo Emerson

If you want others to be happy,

practice compassion.

If you want to be happy,

practice compassion.

—His Holiness the Dalai Lama

Be present in all things and
thankful for all things.

—Maya Angelou

Gratitude turns what we have into enough.

We cannot choose the
day or time when we fully bloom.
It happens in its own time.

—Denis Waitley

Even a snail will eventually

reach its destination.

—Gail Tsukiyama

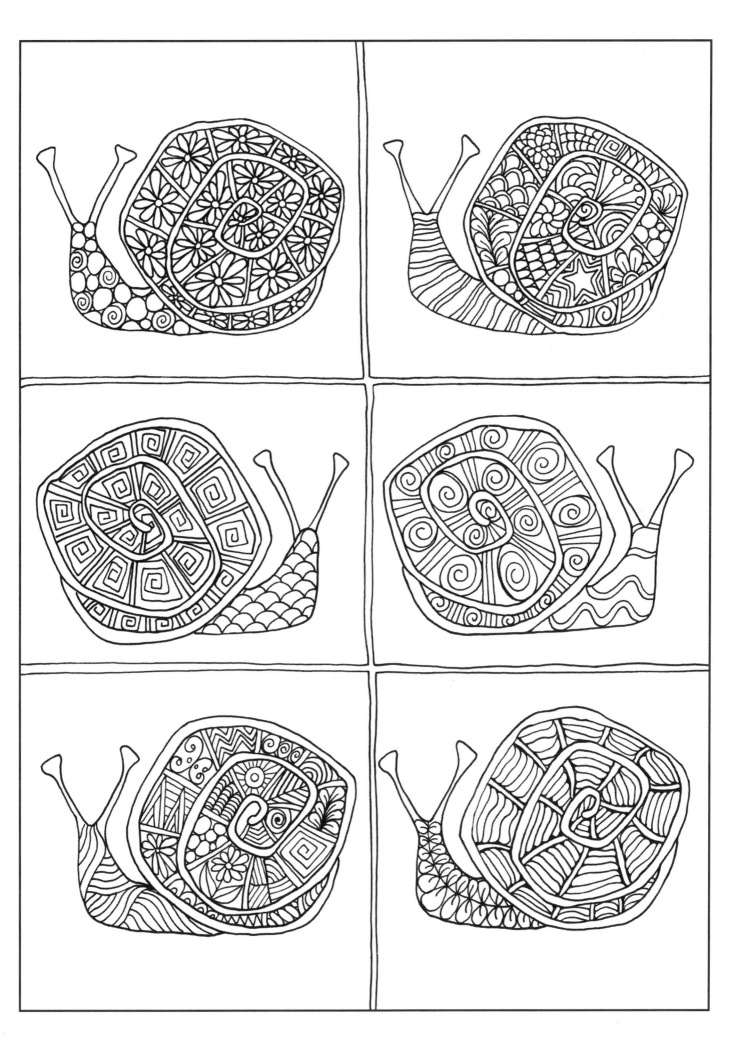

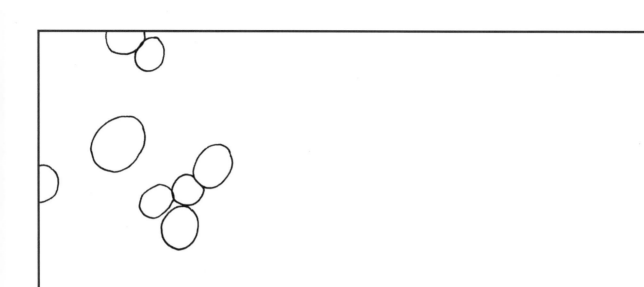

The real voyage of discovery
consists not in seeking new landscapes,
but in having new eyes.

—Marcel Proust

Some people feel the rain;

others just get wet.

—Bob Marley

Happiness is not found in
things you possess, but in what you
have the courage to release.

—Nathaniel Hawthorne

All of the Buddhas of the ages

have been telling you a very simple fact:

Be—don't try to become.

—Osho

Forever is composed of nows.

—Emily Dickinson

You must live in the present,

launch yourself on every wave,

find your eternity in

each moment.

—Henry David Thoreau

Let us be kind to one another,

for most of us are fighting

a hard battle.

—Ian Maclaren

Be wise.
Be kind.
Be true.

Let the beauty of what you love

be what you do.

—Rumi

Be happy in the moment;

that's enough.

Each moment is all we

need, not more.

—Mother Teresa

Somewhere, something incredible

is waiting to be known.

—Sharon Begley

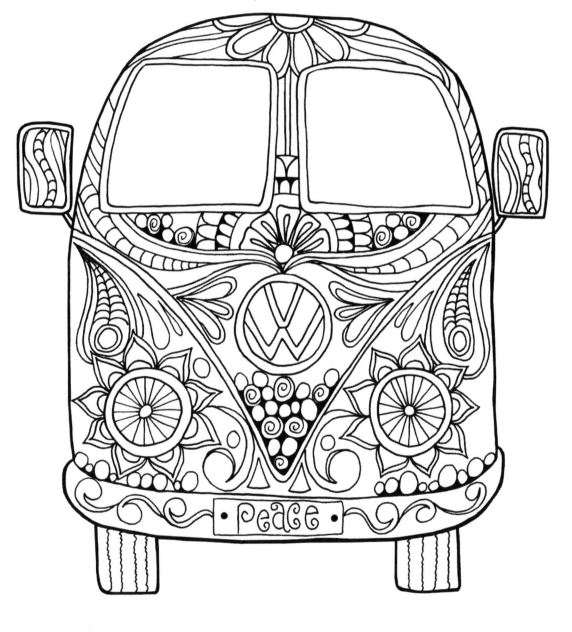

Nature doesn't hurry,

yet everything is accomplished.

—Lao Tzu

There is no way to peace;

there is only peace.

—Mahatma Gandhi

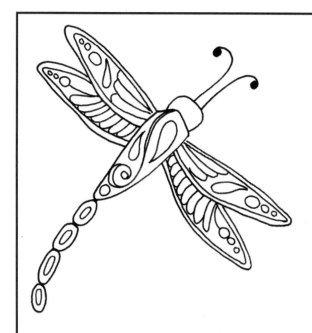

The quieter you become, the

more you can hear.

—Ram Dass

Breathe. Let go.

And remind yourself that

this very moment is the only one

you know you have for sure.

—Oprah Winfrey

Have nothing in your house

that you do not know to be useful,

or believe to be beautiful.

—William Morris

Start where you are.

Use what you have.

—Arthur Ashe

In solitude there is healing.

Speak to your soul. Listen to your heart.

Sometimes in the absence of noise

we find the answers.

—Dodinsky

Don't let people pull you

into their storm.

Pull them into your peace.

—Kimberly Jones

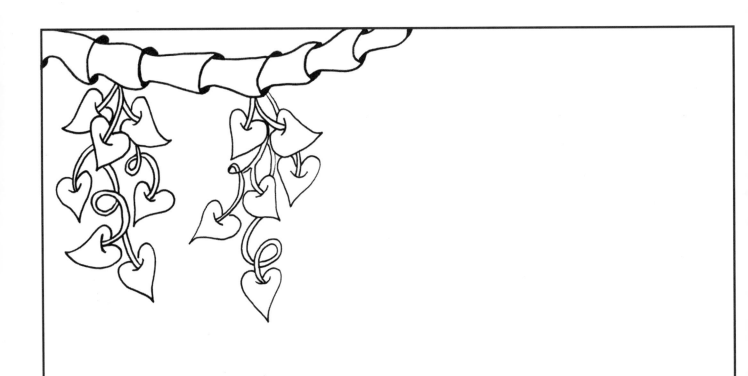

Everything is created twice,

first in the mind and

then in reality.

—Robin Sharma

If you change the way you look at things,

the things you look at change.

—Wayne Dyer

Drink your tea slowly and reverently,

as if it is the axis on which the

whole earth revolves—slowly, evenly,

without rushing toward the future;

live the actual moment.

Only this moment is life.

—Thich Nhat Hanh

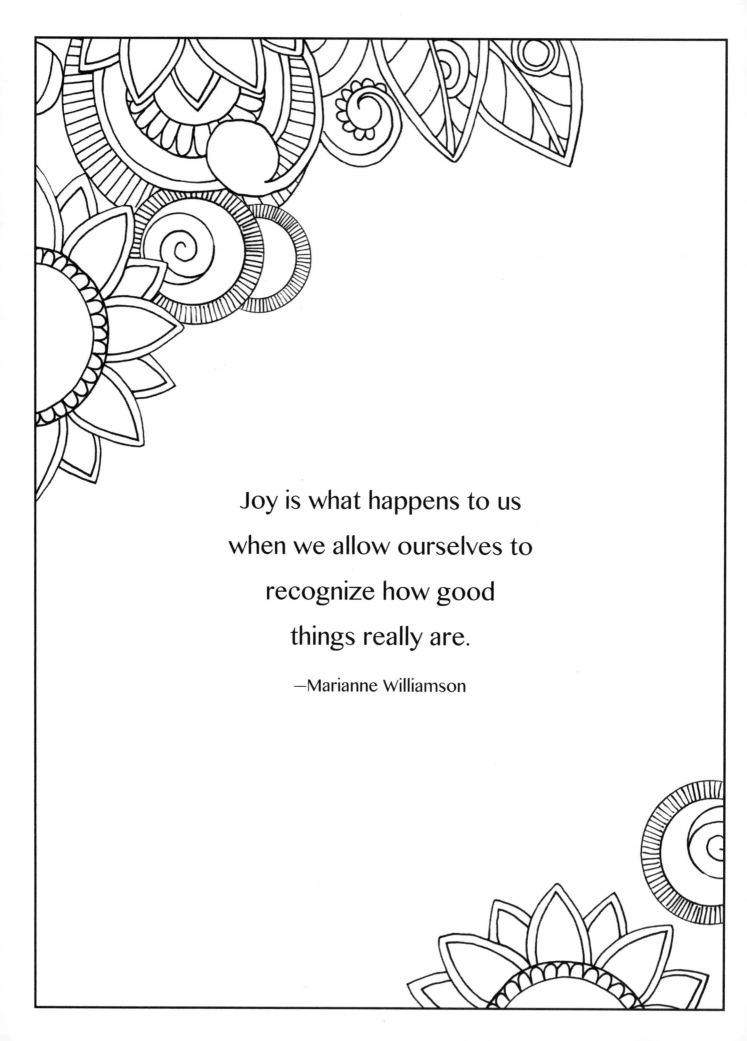

Joy is what happens to us
when we allow ourselves to
recognize how good
things really are.

—Marianne Williamson

We have only this moment,

sparkling like a star in our hand—

and melting like a snowflake.

—Francis Bacon Sr.

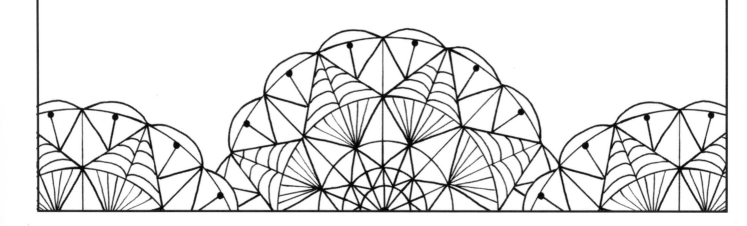

In the end just three things matter:

How well we have lived

How well we have loved

How well we have learned to let go.

—Jack Kornfield

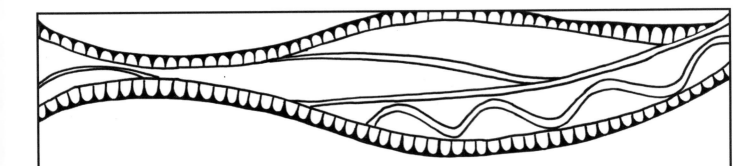

We should all do what

in the long run gives us joy,

even if it is only picking grapes

or sorting the laundry.

—E.B. White

Quiet mind, quiet soul.

—Lailah Gifty Akita

To join or learn more about AARP, visit AARP.org.
For more AARP coloring books, visit
AARP.org/ColoringBooks.

If you like *Inkspirations Mindful Living*,
check out our full line of coloring books:

Inkspirations Create While You Wait

Inkspirations in the Garden

Inkspirations for a Happy Heart

Inkspirations for Women

Inkspirations Animal Kingdom

Inkspirations for Cat Lovers

Inkspirations for Dog Lovers